BANNOCKBURN 1314

BATTLE FOR A NATION

Chris Tabraham

LOMOND
www.lomondbooks.com

D0186405

King Robert Bruce on the Esplanade of Stirling Castle, with the National Wallace Monument beyond.

BANNOCKBURN 1314
BATTLE FOR A NATION

BACKGROUND TO THE BATTLE

King Robert when he heard say
That Englishmen in such array
And in such great quantity
Were come into the land, in haste got he
His men summoned generally,
And they came all willfully
To the Torwood . . .

(from John Barbour's epic poem *The Bruce*, composed in the 1370s)

THE SCOTTISH WARS OF INDEPENDENCE

On Friday 30 March 1296 Edward I of England crossed the Scottish Border near Wark-on-Tweed at the head of a 30,000-strong army and made for Berwick-upon-Tweed, then Scotland's chief town. Two days later two-thirds of its population, some 7500 souls, lay dead. That single act of aggression heralded over 60 years of bloodshed between the two kingdoms – the Scottish Wars of Independence.

The untimely deaths, in relatively quick succession, of two Scottish sovereigns – Alexander III (1286) and Margaret 'the maid of Norway' (1290) – were ultimately what moved King Edward to invade. He sensed an opportunity to end, for good and all, the ambiguous relationship between the crowns of England and Scotland that had rumbled on for more than 200 years – ever since that day in 1072 when Malcolm III of Scotland had bent the knee to William the Conqueror at Abernethy, beside the River Tay east of Perth, and become 'his man'.

Within a month of the brutal attack on Berwick, Edward I defeated the Scots in battle on a wind-swept hill overlooking Dunbar. Scotland now found itself up against one of the most efficient fighting machines in Europe. The English had after all been waging war for most of the preceding century – on Crusade in the Holy Land, in France, against the Irish and the Welsh. The Scots, by contrast, had had little recent experience of warfare.

But the Scots resisted. In those dark early days, William Wallace led the fight-back, achieving his greatest moment on 11 September 1297 at the Battle of Stirling Bridge. Following his cruel death in 1305 at the hands of the merciless Edward I, into his shoes stepped Robert Bruce.

ROBERT BRUCE

Robert Bruce, Earl of Carrick, was enthroned as King of Scots at Scone, near Perth, on Easter Sunday 1306. Within three months, and almost within sight of the Moot Hill on which he had been acclaimed by his people, he was very nearly captured by Edward's leading henchman in Scotland, Sir Aymer de Valence, Earl of Pembroke, whilst planning an assault on the town of Perth. All that coming winter and well into the following spring, Bruce disappeared into the ether, during which time he had his famous encounter with that spider in a cave. When he re-emerged, he exacted immediate

Imposing Stirling Castle atop its rocky perch. So strategic was the royal fortress's position in the Scottish realm that it brought the English here time and again during the bloody Wars of Independence of the 14th century. It was the threat of losing this vital garrison fortress to King Robert Bruce on Midsummer's Day 1314 that brought Edward II in person to Scotland – and to defeat at Bannockburn.

K. Robert (9)
Bruce and his
Second Wyff

King Robert Bruce of Scotland (1306-29) was twice married. Here he is shown with his second queen, Elizabeth, daughter of Richard de Burgh, Earl of Ulster, whom he wed in c.1302. Bruce's father-in-law fought on the English side at Bannockburn.

revenge on Pembroke, routing his cavalry at Loudon Hill, Ayrshire in April 1307.

From Loudon Hill, Bruce's star was in the ascendant. His luck was in almost immediately. On 7 July 1307, Edward I, 'Hammer of the Scots' and Bruce's would-be nemesis, breathed his last beside the Solway Firth, preparing yet again to invade Scotland. Bruce doubtless breathed a huge sigh of relief on hearing that news, knowing only too well how formidable an adversary Edward had been. By the end of that year he had swept up the Great Glen and booted the English out of their bolt-holes in the north. By the end of 1308 he had forced his most feared enemies, the Comyns, to flee the country. Bruce would next encounter the Comyns on the battlefield of Bannockburn.

So strong was the tide running in Bruce's favour that by March 1309 he was presiding over his first parliament, at St. Andrews in the heart of his realm. Now only Lothian lay beyond his reach. Not for much longer. Even as parliament was in session, Bruce had begun to address 'the Lothian Question'. His answer: a powerful combination of the mailed fist and blackmail. By 1311 an impressive list of Lothian landowners had entered Bruce's peace, none more valuable than Sir Robert Keith, Marischal of Scotland. Keith would play a vital role for Bruce on the battlefield of Bannockburn.

Thereafter, Bruce took the fight to the English. Soon the good folk of the northern counties of England were discovering for themselves what Bruce meant when he talked about 'defending himself with the longest stick he had'. Time and again the Scots crossed the Border, to burn and pillage, or to extort blackmail. The raids did far more than quench the thirst for revenge; they replenished Bruce's near-empty war-chest.

EDWARD II

Meanwhile, Edward II, son of the great Edward I, had very different troubles, most of his own making. Almost from his first day on the throne, Edward courted trouble. He ignored his late father's wish that his bones be carried on campaign against the Scots, and instead had them packed off back to London. And although he himself somehow summoned up the courage to enter Scotland that summer, he only made it as far as Cumnock, in Ayrshire, before turning round and heading for home.

Edward didn't abandon his father's ambition of bringing Scotland to heel though. He continued to ensure that the English garrisons holed up in their Scottish castles were well-supplied – so long as they held on to them, of course – and he did what he could to support those Scots continuing to rebel against Bruce. He even mounted another invasion, over the winter of 1310-11, on this occasion reaching as far as Renfrew on the

Clyde. Bruce, recognising only too well that he could never hope to defeat Edward's army in open battle, was content to leave him to it – for now.

Before Edward left Scotland in August 1311, he placed a gentleman by the name of Piers Gaveston in charge of the strategic town of Perth, on the River Tay. But Gaveston, far from helping his king win Scotland, would play a prominent part in Edward losing his own kingdom.

Edward and Gaveston were more than just king and courtier; they were lovers. Edward, despite being married and fathering an heir, had long been infatuated with Gaveston – and just as long been despised by those at court for consorting with such a loathsome individual. They included Edward's own father, who so detested his son's playmate that he banished him from the realm. Now, with his late father's bones still warm, Edward brought Gaveston home; to rub salt in his nobles' wounds, he made him Earl of Cornwall.

Perhaps Edward was just not cut out to be king. He had after all only been fourth in line to the throne. It might have been better all round if one of his elder brothers had survived long enough to ascend the throne. But that was not Edward's lot, and it took the great earls of England five years to separate the despicable Gaveston from their king's presence. In the end, they had to resort to murdering him, in 1312. Edward would soon regret falling foul of the man behind the plot, the powerful Earl of Lancaster, when he began to fund-raise for Bannockburn.

THE PARLEY AT STIRLING

In the summer of 1313 King Robert was on the Isle of Man fighting the English. Things were going well, and on 12 June he captured the castle of Rushen after a brief siege. Meanwhile, back home, his younger brother, Edward, Earl of Carrick, was making far heavier weather of capturing the important Stirling Castle. He had laid siege well before Easter, but here he was,

over three months later, and still no sign of Sir Philip Mowbray, its English keeper, surrendering. It was stalemate.

It was Mowbray who broke the deadlock. Shortly before Midsummer Day (24 June), he rode out through the castle gate and parleyed with Carrick. He made him an offer he couldn't refuse – if Carrick would lift the siege, Mowbray would undertake to keep his men in the castle. And if, by Midsummer Day 1314, no English army had advanced to within a league, that is 3 miles, of the castle, then Mowbray would surrender unconditionally.

The offer was certainly tempting. Rather than continue idling away their time in siege camp, Carrick and his men would be free to serve King Robert's cause more productively elsewhere. And so Carrick accepted Mowbray's offer. It only remained for their respective sovereigns to be informed. Carrick despatched messengers to Man, whilst Mowbray hastened south to England. When King Robert I and King Edward II received the news, each knew instinctively what that Stirling parley would lead to – showdown.

King Edward II of England (1307-27) is shown here receiving the adulation of his people, but in reality he was among the most loathed of English monarchs, thanks in part to his predilection for unsuitable 'male favourites', such as the despicable Hugh Despenser the younger, who fought at Bannockburn.

BUILD-UP TO THE BATTLE

Armed well in all his gear
[Bruce] plunged into the ditch, and with his spear
Tested it as he waded over;
Up to his neck stood the water.

We do not know where Bruce was when he received the news of the parley at Stirling, but we do know that he was not best pleased with his brother. Had he not spent the last six years successfully avoiding a pitched battle with the English? Even during Edward's fruitless invasion of 1310-11, Bruce had let his adversary roam around Scotland comparatively unmolested, confident that in the end he would run out of food and fodder. Risking a set-piece confrontation when it wasn't necessary would have been rash at the very least, disastrous at worst. Now, thanks to his brother's parley, that daunting prospect was all the more likely. But the deal had been made, and Bruce was honour-bound to accept.

Meantime there was a kingdom still to be won. Despite the successes of the past seven years, pockets of resistance yet remained, most disturbingly in the south-east. By now Bruce had made significant progress persuading its inhabitants, by fair means and foul, to come into his peace, but it was an uphill struggle whilst the English continued to hold sway from their castles. They had large garrisons in three of Scotland's greatest royal strongholds – Berwick, Roxburgh and Edinburgh – and held a string of lesser strengths from Jedburgh, hard by the Border, to Dirleton on the Firth of Forth. Individually each was strong; collectively they were formidable.

The greatest prize, Berwick, would surely have fallen to Bruce himself on a December night in 1312, had the guards not been alerted by a wretched dog barking at the crucial moment when his forces were stealthily climbing the town walls on rope ladders. Next he unleashed his trusty captains on the other two English strongholds – Roxburgh and Edinburgh. 'The Good Sir James' of Douglas, Bruce's closest friend, and Thomas Randolph, Earl of Moray, Bruce's nephew, had learnt much from the attempt on Berwick, relying not on siege but subterfuge. Douglas took Roxburgh on the night of 19 February 1314, his men climbing their rope ladders and catching the garrison completely off-guard; the choice of date, Fastern's Eve (Shrove Tuesday), was inspired, for Guillemin de Fenes and his garrison were making the most of their last chance to party before the Lenten fast. Lent was still in force when Moray took Edinburgh by a similar stratagem on 14 March 1314. Now Berwick alone remained in English hands – and Stirling too, of course. From now on Bruce would have to focus his energies on the latter.

The chroniclers are silent as to how Edward received the news of the parley at Stirling. He would certainly have had mixed emotions. The memory of his last, abortive invasion would still be fresh; that and the supreme difficulty he had raising a reasonable force for the fray from his most-unreasonable earls. Now that poor Piers Gaveston was dead, Edward and his nobles had reached an understanding – after a fashion;

King Robert Bruce (1306-29) mounted on his 'grey': the equestrian statue at Bannockburn. Bruce had fought for Edward I prior to his enthronement and knew all too well just how formidable a fighting machine the English army was. For the first seven years of his reign he carefully avoided engaging them in pitched battle, resorting to 'scorched-earth' and 'hit-and-run' tactics. However, he knew he would have to confront them one day if he was to secure his throne and his country's independence.

The pivotal importance of Stirling Castle (circled) is demonstrated in this 13th-century map of Britain, if somewhat over dramatically. Stirling has been described as 'like a huge brooch clasping Lowlands and Highlands together'.

requiring them to attend him at Berwick on 10 June next. From Easter 1314 order upon order issued from his royal chancery, as the preparations gathered momentum. The northern and midland shires of England were to provide infantrymen and archers, Bristol and Wales were to send crossbowmen, whilst a 28-strong fleet of ships was to be assembled to supply the land army from the sea. Knights from Ireland, France, Aquitaine, Poitou, Gascony and Germany were summonsed to fight on the battlefield of Bannockburn, alongside Sir Giles D'Argentan, now released from gaol and on his voyage home.

Just how many men answered Edward's call to muster at Wark-on-Tweed on 10 June 1314 is not known. There should have been upwards of 22,000 had they all turned up. But not all did and, most critically for Edward, counted among the absentees were the majority of his own earls; clearly the ending of Gaveston's life had not ended the feud between the king and his most senior subjects. Of the eight earls invited to join Edward at Newminster Abbey, near Morpeth, in late May, five never showed; Lancaster, Warwick, Arundel, Surrey and Oxford all presented their excuses and sent only token forces in their place.

So it was that Edward set out for Scotland accompanied only by Humphrey de Bohun, Earl of Hereford and Constable of England, Gilbert de Clare, Earl of Gloucester, and the ever-loyal Pembroke. Riding alongside them was Richard de Burgh, Earl of Ulster and Bruce's own father-in-law, and one Scottish earl, Robert de Umfraville, Earl of Angus, who despite his title was a Northumbrian.

We have no way of knowing what thoughts raced through Bruce's mind as the countdown to Midsummer Day 1314 began. He doubtless harboured the hope that somehow his adversary would never make it to within a league of Stirling Castle in the time allotted in the parley, and so lose the fortress by default. Thereby he would avoid a direct confrontation in a pitched battle against the much larger English army.

when Edward and Lancaster celebrated their newfound bond at a banquet, they still found it necessary to dine at separate tables!

If Edward harboured any misgivings about proceeding against Bruce, he soon laid them aside. In August 1313 he wrote to the Empress of Constantinople pleading for the release from his prison in Salonika of Sir Giles d'Argentan, 'the third best knight in Christendom' (Bruce himself was acknowledged as the first). She agreed, and Edward rejoiced at the news. Little did he know that he would owe his life to his bold knight on the battlefield of Bannockburn.

By Christmas-tide 1313, the laborious process of gathering his army had begun in earnest. Edward issued writs for military service on his eight earls and 87 barons,

But he had to assume the worst. Bruce therefore ordered his army to rendezvous in the Torwood by the middle of May.

The Torwood was a large expanse of dense forest lying some 7 miles (11 km) to the south of Stirling Castle, along the road to Falkirk. If Edward wished to relieve Stirling, he would have to come by there. The ancient wood was an old haunt. In the dark days following Wallace's defeat at Falkirk in 1298, Bruce and his fellow guardians of the realm of Scotland had sheltered therein to carry on the business of government. The Torwood had served its purpose then; it would serve again now.

The Torwood suited Bruce's needs perfectly. Not only did its forest canopy afford valuable cover for his troops, it also had areas of open rocky ground where they could train and practice manoeuvres. Moreover, it had an escape route – the hills and broken country to the west. Bruce was leaving his options open – stay and fight, or beat a tactical withdrawal.

They came from all over the country, and beyond, to the Torwood that month of May. Bruce's brother, Carrick, came with the men of Galloway. Moray brought the men of the north and Nithsdale, and Douglas the men of Strathclyde and the eastern Borders. Keith, the Marischal, would command the cavalry of light horse, and Bruce himself the men of Carrick, Argyll and the Isles, ably assisted by Angus Óg MacDonald; 'wee Angus' would be a tower of strength come the day.

Morale must have been high in the Torwood, what with the capture of Roxburgh and Edinburgh still fresh in their minds. As they gathered in that great wood, tales would be told and retold around the campfires of those exploits – of how Sim 'of the Ledhows' had been the first to scale Roxburgh's battlements and 'stykit with ane knyff' the sentry who would otherwise have roused the garrison from their wassailing; and of William Francis, who had led the assault on Edinburgh, inching his way up the precipitous rock in the pitch darkness by a route he had come to know

The Scottish army that fought at Bannockburn comprised men from all corners of the realm. They included 5,000 Gaels from the Hebrides and Western Isles, who came to the muster in the Torwood under the banner of their chief, Angus Óg MacDonald, grandson of the eponymous Donald. This 13th-century gravestone of Gilbride, chief of the MacKinnons, on Iona shows how their leaders were armed for the fight – a simple pointed basinet (helmet) over an aventail of chain mail, a triangular shield and single-handed sword. Robert Bruce himself commanded Angus Óg's Islesmen on the second day of the battle.

as a lad in the castle garrison when sneaking out to meet his sweetheart.

But most popular of all would have been the tales of their great king leading from the front, as he did that 'myrk nycht' in January 1313 when he waded up to his neck through the icy waters of Perth's great ditch to regain that strategic town. But Bruce himself knew only too

The cream of Edward of England's army was his cavalry. This image of Sir Geoffrey Luttrell, from his early 14th-century Luttrell Psalter, *shows how these mounted knights would have looked on the day of the battle – in full armour sitting astride his destrier, or war-horse, with sword in hand. His wife prepares to hand him his helmet and lance, and his daughter-in-law his shield. Rider and horse are both brightly emblazoned with the knight's coat of arms.*

well that morale alone didn't win battles. They were in the Torwood not to reminisce about what had been, but to train for what might be – pitched battle against the might of England's chivalry. And so they trained, and trained hard – and the hardest thing they trained at was 'forming the schiltron'.

Schiltrum or schiltron simply means 'shield-ring' and was the basic formation of the Scottish infantry. Unlike the English, who relied mostly on great knights mounted on their heavy horses to carry the day, the Scots depended heavily on their foot-soldiers armed with iron-tipped spears up to 16 ft long. These spearmen were deployed in large schiltrons, each holding in excess of 500 men, that would move slowly about the battlefield like some enormous hedgehog with its bristles fully exposed. The principle was simple enough: a horse charging headlong towards such a formation will instinctively stop the moment it

reaches the barricade of spears, thereby causing mêlée and confusion. The length of the spear was critical, for it had to be capable of reaching the body of the horse before the advancing knight's lance pierced the man wielding the spear.

When all those summonned assembled were
He [Edward] had of fighters with him there . . .
Many a worthy man and wycht [bold]
And many a richly attired knight
And many a sturdy frisky steed
Arrayed in all its finest weed [armour]

Whilst Bruce was in the Torwood overseeing military manoeuvres, Edward was grappling with a very different problem – how to get 2,500 heavy cavalry, and 15,000 infantry, and all their paraphernalia from the mustering-point at Wark-on-Tweed to Stirling Castle in under two weeks.

The English side of the Tweed, from Wark Castle down river past Norham to opposite Berwick, must have been a sight to behold that early June as Edward's great army came from all the airts to gather there under the warm June sun in preparation for the invasion. The summer air would have been thick with the sounds of thousands of infantrymen being barked at by their constables in the only language they knew, shouting. It would have been thick too with the snorting of horses as the impressive array of mounted knights arrived, each with his own entourage of squires and attendants, field-pavilions and finery. It would have been thick too with the noises of the smiths and sutlers, wagonners and wheelwrights, fletchers and farriers, priests, prostitutes and the rest, going about their various businesses.

They should have crossed into Scotland on Monday 10 June but last-minute demands for more troops had led to delay. It was Monday 17 June before the order to advance was given. That left just seven days to get to within a league of Stirling, barely a week for Edward to secure his last great garrison in central Scotland.

Edward, advised by the Earl of Pembroke, opted to take the more direct route, up Lauderdale and across the Lammermuir Hills to Edinburgh, a distance of 20 leagues (60 miles/96 km), rather than the longer but more

easily graded route up the coast from Berwick. By that first nightfall they had reached Earlston, by the next they had gained Soutra, and by the third they were in Edinburgh, and a welcome rendezvous with the fleet. And there they rested for two whole days, whilst the huge baggage-train was replenished. Then it was on the move once more, for the remaining 13 leagues (40 miles/64 km) via Falkirk to Stirling.

Oh how that very name – Falkirk – would have gladdened the hearts of the veterans marching in Edward's army that day. Hereford the Constable had been just a lad riding behind his father on the July day in 1298 when the 'Hammer of the Scots' exacted bloody revenge for Wallace's victory at Stirling Bridge. Now here he was, commanding the army himself, riding along with his young nephew, Henry de Bohun, by his side, no doubt regaling him with a blow-by-blow account of that victorious encounter. Did those stories and deeds of derring-do perhaps inspire the young lad to the rashness we shall find him perpetrating in those opening moments on the battlefield of Bannockburn?

Falkirk was reached in under 24 hours thanks to those memories, and the fact that, with Midsummer Day fast approaching, the sky barely got dark. The morrow, 23 June, would bring them within a league of Stirling. Edward would have achieved his goal.

THE COMBATANTS AND BATTLE ORDER

THE SCOTTISH ARMY

Commander-in-Chief
King Robert I – aged 39

Four 'battles' or brigades,
each 1,000 – 1,500 strong (mostly infantry)

First Battle – commander
King Robert I

Second Battle – commander
Sir Edward Bruce, Earl of Carrick

Third Battle – commander
Sir Thomas Randolph, Earl of Moray

Fourth Battle – commander
Sir James, Lord of Douglas

Cavalry of 500 light horse – commander
Sir Robert Keith, Marischal of Scotland

Total no. of fighting men – between 7,000
and 10,000 (estimate only)

THE ENGLISH ARMY

Commander-in-Chief
King Edward II – aged 30

Ten 'battles' or brigades, each comprising
a mixture of cavalry and infantry

Fore-Battle (Vanguard) – joint commanders
Sir Humphrey de Bohun, Earl of Hereford
and Constable of England, and Sir Gilbert
de Clare, Earl of Gloucester

Main-Battle (Centre) – commander
King Edward II

Subordinate commanders included
Sir Aymer de Valence, Earl of Pembroke;
Sir Giles d'Argentan; Sir Henry Beaumont;
Sir Maurice Berkeley; Sir Robert Clifford;
Sir John Comyn; Sir William Daynecourt;
Sir Hugh Despenser the younger;
Sir Edmund de Mauley; Sir Pain Tiptoft;
Sir Marmaduke Tweng; Sir Ingram d'Umfraville;
Sir Robert de Umfraville

Total no. of fighting men – up to 2,500 cavalry
and upwards of 15,000 infantry (estimate only)

THE SCOTTISH ARMY
WHAT THEY LOOKED LIKE

KNIGHT: Not used like his English counterpart because he didn't normally have access to the heavy horse (destrier). He rode a lighter 'hobby-horse', from which he derived his name of 'hobelar'; this could carry the same weight but didn't have the speed. He was armed with a light lance, sword and perhaps a battle-axe or mace, and was heavily protected by armour – helmet, plate armour and chain mail – worn over a thickly padded jacket (gambeson). Over his body armour he wore a surcoat displaying his heraldic arms. His leather-covered wooden shield was similarly decorated.

INFANTRYMAN: The infantry did the bulk of the fighting. A typical infantryman eschewed full body armour, finding it too much of an encumbrance. He wore a cap of steel or leather, a quilted jacket (aketon) possibly with some crude plate armour or mail for added protection, and gloves of plate. He was armed with an iron-tipped spear between 12 ft and 16 ft long. He also had a knife and either a battle-axe or sword. He normally didn't carry a shield, needing both hands free for his spear.

ARCHER: A relatively new addition to the fighting force, each archer probably carried a longbow and a quiver holding 24 arrows, though some may have wielded the short bow.

THE ENGLISH ARMY
WHAT THEY LOOKED LIKE

KNIGHT: The main-stay of the English army. In battle he rode a heavy horse, or 'destrier', which could carry all the weight of its armoured rider and still gallop fast. When not in battle order, he rode a smaller horse, or 'palfrey', which gave a more comfortable ride. In battle he carried a heavy lance around 14 ft long which he wielded 'couched', that is, gripped tightly under the arm and clasped to the ribcage. In most other respects his appearance was similar to his Scottish counterpart.

INFANTRYMAN: Like his Scottish counterpart he wore a helmet of some sort, a 'kettle hat' or skull cap perhaps, a hauberk or padded jacket (gambeson), and a round shield, or targe. He might carry a weapon for thrusting, such as a pike or bill, but more commonly a shafted axe some 5 ft long which could smash plate armour.

ARCHER: Similar to his Scottish counterpart.

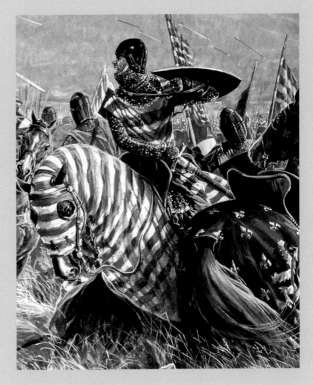

THE BATTLE
- DAY ONE -

(SUNDAY 23 JUNE 1314)

On Sunday then in the morn
Quite soon after the rise of the sun
They [the Scots] heard their mass communally
And many shrived themselves devoutly
Who thought they would die in that mêlée
Or there to make their country free.

DAWN

Dawn on Sunday 23 June found Bruce and his army not in the Torwood but a mile or so to the north in the New Park, part of the royal hunting forest lying within the shadow of Stirling Castle. Around noon the previous day, spies had brought intelligence that the English 'with mekill mycht' (great might) had reached Edinburgh and were advancing on Stirling. The moment of truth was drawing ever closer.

Bruce had straightway ordered his troops to break camp and withdraw beyond the Bannock Burn, a good-sized stream running east and north into the muddy flats of the River Forth. They were to reform in the shelter of the New Park. The Roman road along which Edward's army would have to march passed over the Bannock Burn and through the Park.

All that Saturday they had waited there, Moray in the vanguard, nearest the castle, Carrick and Douglas with the young Walter Stewart in the centre, and Bruce commanding the rearguard, closest to the enemy. Bruce was still keeping his options open – stand and fight or melt into the mist. His men were not left idle. Bruce had ordered them to dig pits, hundreds of them, in the ground along the north bank of the Bannock Burn, either side of the road to Stirling. Each was to be 'a foot in diameter and as deep as a man's knee, so thickly placed they could be compared to a wax-comb that bees make'. Concealed by sticks and grass, those pits would serve as booby-traps for the heavy English destriers and their haughty armoured riders.

Around dawn on Sunday, the men were roused from their slumbers by their sergeants and ordered to attend mass. What a sight and sound that must have been – upward of 7,000 men kneeling there among the trees, mumbling their confessions before God, each knowing full well that this day, the eve of the feast day of the Nativity of St. John the Baptist, might be his last on God's earth. The mass over, Bruce instructed that each man arm himself for the coming fight and go to his allotted station. The day being a fast day, each man knew he would have to remain there, and do battle if needs be, on a near-empty stomach of bread and water.

With the men dismissed, Bruce turned to Douglas and Keith and asked them to take a mounted scouting party and assess the situation in the English camp. Decision-time was fast approaching.

Meanwhile dawn in the English camp at

The defining moment on Day One of the great battle – King Robert Bruce (left), mounted on his small 'grey' and wearing his gold coronet and surcoat bearing the royal arms of Scotland, prepares to bring his battle-axe down on the visored helm of Sir Henry de Bohun, nephew of the hereditary Constable of England, shown riding his destrier (war-horse) and emblazoned from helm to toe with the arms of the de Bohun Earls of Hereford.

Edward II and his entourage of mounted knights spent each night of the march from Wark-on-Tweed in their brightly-coloured pavilions (campaign tents). Much of the huge baggage-train was devoted to transporting these and their owners' other equipment.

Falkirk that Sunday found Edward in the comparative snugness of his silk pavilion-tent stirring from his night's slumbers. The previous day had been another strenuous ride along the road from Edinburgh, a distance of 8 leagues (24 miles/37 km). But the two-day rest at Edinburgh had restored aching limbs and refreshed equally exhausted horses, and the route had been flat and the weather warm.

Here too the spectacle was wondrous to behold, as the 20,000-strong English army prepared to set out on their last short leg to Stirling Castle. Knights at their toilet ensured they looked their best for the coming fray, the squires laying out their shining armour and their minions striking the tents and stowing their masters' cherished possessions onto the baggage train for one last haul. Out from the ironbound chests came the embroidered banners, standards and pennons that would flout the sky that day, each one emblazoned with its master's colourful coat of arms. Out too came the destriers, the heavy horses hitherto unsaddled and unridden but now groomed and prepared to bear their masters into battle, leaving the hard-pressed palfreys to get much needed rest. And all around them the sounds of the constables barking out their orders, and the nervous laughter of the men as it gradually dawned on them what perhaps lay in store that day. They too would have to march, and maybe fight, on rumbling stomachs, because of the vigil for the feast day of the Nativity of St. John the Baptist.

Douglas and Keith witnessed all this feverish activity from a safe distance. They were aghast at the awesome spectacle, of 'the largest and boldest host in Christendom' moving along the dusty road towards Stirling, the baggage-train reaching back, it was said, almost to the outskirts of Edinburgh. But amidst the array of shining shields, burnished helmets, and brightly coloured banners, there was one vital detail

HOW A SCHILTRON WORKS

A body of foot-soldiers armed with long spears form a line and the men at the end turn back the way until they touch, thus forming a rough circle. Other concentric rings of foot-soldiers then form around that circle, the principle being that the thicker the circle, the more difficult it is to breach. The outer ring then kneels, and sets its spear ends at an angle into the ground so that the murderous tips point obliquely out beyond the shield-ring at about the height of a horse's neck. The rows of spearmen behind crouch or stand, holding their spears more horizontally, level with a horse's chest.

The sergeants stationed within the circle shout at and cajole their men to preserve the circle, and goad them in the required direction. If men fall, their places are taken by reserves from inside the circle. For the schiltron is not a dense mass of men; its centre is left relatively clear. From here its commander can control it, and here any captured enemy can be brought, a herald confirming whether the poor chap is worth sparing for ransom or better dead!

A schiltron was therefore quite a simple formation, but it would have taken many hours of training by each commander and every sergeant and man in the schiltron to get it absolutely right. High on the training schedule, no doubt, would have been to get each man used to the sheer horror of standing there armed only with a long bit of wood as 2 tons of armoured horseflesh thundered towards him.

Robert Bruce (centre) looks on from his position in the New Park as Moray's brigade engages Sir Robert Clifford's cavalry in the afternoon of Day One of the battle. The mighty castle of Stirling looms in the background.

they could not have made out – the divisions beginning to manifest themselves in Edward's command headquarters.

Throughout the two-week march from Wark-on-Tweed, Pembroke had guided Edward's army. Now, as the hour of battle approached, Edward relieved him of that burden. But instead of bestowing the command of the vanguard on Hereford, for some unaccountable reason he invited Gloucester to share in that command. Hereford felt snubbed. Had not de Bohuns, hereditary Constables of England, been leading the country's armies into battle for generations? How come now, with the real prospect of a de Bohun leading England to overwhelming victory over the Scots, Edward should appoint a nobleman 15 years Hereford's junior, and with no credentials as a commander, to share his hour of glory? Was Gloucester being rewarded perhaps for supporting Edward during those dark days when Piers Gaveston was alive and

fomenting rebellion among the great nobles of England? The cracks so thinly papered over following Gaveston's death were beginning to emerge once more. Yet the king had spoken – and that was the end of the matter.

AFTERNOON

Edward's army was by now strung out along the road to Stirling. Such was Gloucester's youthful impetuosity that the vanguard had long forded the Carron Water and crossed over Stanehouse Muir to the Torwood, leaving Edward and the main battle group trailing in their wake. Along the way they passed a lone horseman – Sir Philip Mowbray, keeper of Stirling, galloping south to rendezvous with his sovereign.

Edward heard Mowbray out. Now that his liege lord had come within a league of the castle, England's honour had been saved. Mowbray would now be able to reprovision his beleaguered garrison, and welcome his majesty within the castle. Edward was in a quandary – proceed unchallenged to Stirling, or attempt to engage the Scots in pitched battle. His decision was immaterial. Thanks to hot-headed Gloucester, the die had already been cast.

By now the English vanguard had put the darkened Torwood behind them and were headed for the Bannock Burn. As they cantered down towards the stream they glimpsed ahead of them, across the valley, a body of Scots shaping as if to withdraw into the New Park. Scarce believing their luck, Gloucester, Hereford and their fellow knights pricked their destriers into action. Splashing over the Bannock Burn they galloped up the slope towards the retreating foe.

One knight managed to outrace his fellows, his blue and yellow heraldic colours emblazoned with six lions marking him out as young Henry de Bohun, Hereford's nephew. Henry's adrenaline was pumping. Not only was he, a de Bohun, leading the cavalry charge, as was only right, he had glimpsed through his visor a Scottish knight mounted on a small 'grey' a little apart from the rest. The golden crown atop his helm told him all he need know – that there in his sights was none other than the king of Scots himself. He rode full tilt towards his prey. But as they closed, Bruce adroitly swerved, avoided the impact and, standing in his stirrups, twisted round and smashed his axe down on de Bohun's helmet, cleaving it and the young man's head in two.

Bruce's men, looking on in admiration, cheered and surged from their cover to engage the onrushing cavalry. The impetuous Gloucester was among the first to be unhorsed, and within a short time he and his comrades

had deserted the field. Bruce dismounted and took the plaudits of his men. All he could say in reply was: 'Look what he did to my axe!'

Oblivious to this embarrassing reverse, Edward, still undecided, had meanwhile dispatched Clifford with a troop of 300 horse to reconnoitre the ground ahead, in an attempt to find a route through to the castle that did not involve threading through the New Park. They too crossed the Bannock Burn but, avoiding the New Park, they steered a course across the open carse, between the Park and the tidal mud flats of the Forth. They had almost made it past the Park unseen when Moray, closest to Stirling,

Robert Bruce slays Sir Henry de Bohun – the opening action on Day One. This 15th-century illustration is one of the earliest depictions of Bruce's great victory.

Both armies marched to Bannockburn accompanied by their clergy bearing holy relics, to aid them in their hour of need. Foremost among the Scottish relics was the 8th-century Brecbennoch (now the Monymusk Reliquary), pictured above, believed to contain relics of St. Columba; it is probable that the 3 inch (90 mm) high wooden casket was housed within a larger decorated box to enable the soldiers to see it as they prayed before going into battle.

ordered his brigade to engage the enemy. The schiltron was soon formed and braced for the coming impact. Now was the moment of truth for all that hard training in the Torwood during the merry month of May.

A bloody and bruising encounter ensued. At one point Douglas pleaded with Bruce to let him go to Moray's aid, but Bruce, fearful of committing more of his precious troops, would hear none of it: 'As Our Lord sees me, you shall not go one foot towards him. If he does well, let him take well.' So the two of them watched from the safety of the Park as the horse and the 'hedgehog' on the carse below them engaged. At the first contact the leading horses reared up, twisting and turning to steer clear of the thrusting spears. Sir William Deyncourt and Sir Thomas Grey were among the first to fall prey to the advancing schiltron; Deyncourt was killed outright, but Grey was dragged into the schiltron and held for ransom. Soon the air was thick with dust, and alive with the cries of the stricken. Moray's schiltron held, and the English knights, despairing of ever breaking it, were reduced to hurling their swords and maces into it – to no avail. Clifford, like Gloucester, had no option but to beat a hasty retreat. With dusk descending, 'day one' of the battle of Bannockburn had run its course.

NIGHTFALL

SUNDAY 23 – MONDAY 24 JUNE 1314

DOWN ON THE CARSE

By the time Clifford's bedraggled troop returned to the main battle group, daylight was all but over. It was certainly over as far as further fighting was concerned. The critical thing now was to make camp for the night, and try, as best they could, to rest before the coming dawn. The question was – where?

The priority for the English was their precious destriers; brushing, exercising, watering and feeding them into fine fettle. And so they recrossed the Bannock Burn and made for the lower carse, where there was sufficient dry ground both to accommodate their pavilions and to groom and graze the horses; the water in the sluggish pools would suffice for the thirsty stallions. The infantry and the baggage-train could remain south of the Bannock Burn, each man left to find a place to sleep amid the churned-up mud.

No one could have slept much that night. For the few who had engaged the enemy that day, the sight of the flower of English chivalry being reduced to a ragged rabble by a mass of spear-wielding Scots would have filled them with foreboding. For the many who had had no sight of the action, the sad story of de Bohun's brutal demise would have reminded them of their own mortality.

And so there they camped for the night, incapable of deep sleep for fear of being attacked.

IN THE NEW PARK

In the shelter of the New Park, the Scottish mood was one of muted jubilation. Bruce had once again led from the front, and the schiltron had passed its test with flying colours. Booty there had been, and a handsome ransom or two.

Bruce, though, remained apprehensive. He had spent the last seven years avoiding

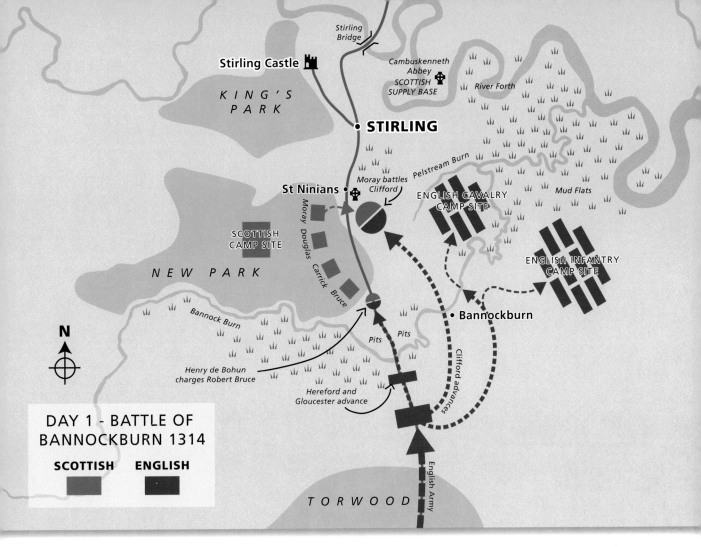

DAY 1 - BATTLE OF BANNOCKBURN 1314

SCOTTISH   ENGLISH

Labels on map: Stirling Bridge; Stirling Castle; KING'S PARK; Cambuskenneth Abbey SCOTTISH SUPPLY BASE; River Forth; STIRLING; Pelstream Burn; Moray battles Clifford; ENGLISH CAVALRY CAMP SITE; Mud Flats; St Ninians; Moray; Douglas; Carrick; Bruce; SCOTTISH CAMP SITE; NEW PARK; ENGLISH INFANTRY CAMP SITE; N; Bannock Burn; Henry de Bohun charges Robert Bruce; Pits; Pits; Bannockburn; Clifford advances; Hereford and Gloucester advance; English Army; TORWOOD

confrontation with the armed might of England in a pitched battle, yet he could so easily throw away all that he had achieved at one fell swoop. From the moment he had called the muster in the Torwood he had kept his options open; they were still available to him. The temptation to stand and fight was strong, the more so after that day's momentous events. But so too was the inclination to withdraw in the night, to head west into the lands of the mountained Lennox glens and carry on the fight in a terrain more suited to him.

As Bruce wrestled with his dilemma, an event occurred that tipped the balance. In the dead of night a lone knight crept out from the English camp and made for the New Park. The sentries, realising that this was no offensive action, let him pass. Sir Alexander Seton of that Ilk, a Scottish lord who had thrown in his lot with England, had become profoundly disillusioned at

the divisions in Edward's headquarters and had come to offer his services. More importantly he had brought intelligence. 'Sire', he implored, 'now is the time if ever you mean to win Scotland. The English have lost heart, they are demoralised and anticipate nothing but a sudden open attack. I swear, on my head and on pain of being hanged and drawn, that if you attack them in the morning you will defeat them easily without loss.'

Seton's words decided Bruce – he would stand and fight. Putting his decision to Carrick, Moray, Douglas and Keith, they replied as one:

Good king, without more delay,
Tomorrow as you see the day
Get all ready for the battle;
For fear of death we shall not fail,
Nor shall any effort refused be
Till we have made our country free.

Map showing the disposition of the two armies, and the action, on Day One of the great battle.

THE BATTLE
- DAY TWO -
(MONDAY 24 JUNE 1314)

[The English] the hard field on horse have taken
All ready to give battle
Arrayed in all their apparel.

Robert Bruce (arms: red lion rampant) leads his army into battle on Day Two, flanked by Douglas (white mullets / stars), Carrick (blue lion rampant), and Keith (red and yellow vertical stripes). An English shield bearing the red cross of St. George lies trampled underfoot.

The English were the first to stir. As the pale sun appeared above the eastern horizon, and in the chilly early morning mist, the sergeants on the south side of the Bannock Burn went among their men, rousing them out of their fitful slumbers. To the north of the burn Edward's knights set about the laborious business of preparing for battle, but not until the bishops, priests and vicars had attended to the most important business of the day – saying mass; for this day was the feast day of the Nativity of St. John the Baptist.

Map showing the disposition of the two armies, and the action, on Day Two of the great battle

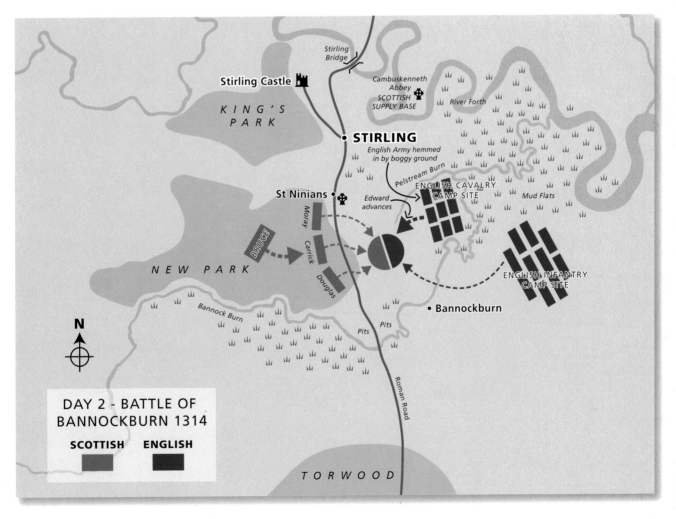

The Scots, newly emerged from their cover in the New Park, kneel and say the Lord's Prayer, each man commending his soul to God, before engaging with the enemy on Day Two of the great battle.

At least, with mass out of the way, both knights and men would be able to break their fast with something more substantial than bread and water.

As the sun rose higher into the pale blue sky, so Edward's army gradually came to order. What Edward's course of action was is not recorded by the chroniclers, but it would seem he had determined on a march in strength northward across the dry carse to Stirling Castle, thereby skirting the New Park. After all, and notwithstanding the events of the previous day, barely a tenth of his army had engaged with the enemy. He still had at his disposal 2,500 mounted knights and upwards of 15,000 infantry.

By mid-morning Edward's army were assembled, awaiting the order to advance. Edward himself led the main battle, sitting astride his heavily armoured destrier, its reins entrusted to the Earl of Pembroke and Sir Giles d'Argentan. Ahead of him, a league hence, loomed Stirling Castle perched atop its rocky craig.

To his left, between him and the New Park, was the vanguard, its quarrelling commanders, Gloucester and Hereford, ready to put aside their differences to protect their sovereign should the need arise. Behind him was the rearguard. The archers were there too, on the flanks, to aid their haughty knights. The seething mass of infantry was still south of the Bannock Burn. Edward had decided that this day would be a day for the 'Flower of England's Chivalry', not for the humble foot-slogger. And so Edward's army advanced at a steady pace north towards Stirling.

[The Scots] all went forth in good array
And took the field full openly,
Many a good man strong and hardy
That were filled of great bounty [courage].

Meanwhile, in the New Park, Bruce and his men too awoke from their sleep, and likewise heard mass from their holy men; the two nations might be bitterly divided politically, but they were united in their religion. Bruce then went forth from his pavilion to rouse his men for the coming fight. His faithful chancellor, Abbot Bernard of Arbroath, who would in due course earn undying fame as the author of the famous Declaration of Arbroath, recorded his words for posterity:

'My Lords, my people, accustomed to enjoy that full freedom for which in times gone by the kings of Scotland have fought many a battle! For eight years or more I have struggled with much labour for my right to the kingdom and for honourable liberty. I have lost brothers, friends and kinsmen. Your own kinsmen have been made captive, and bishops and priests are locked in prison. Our country's nobility has poured forth its blood in war.

Those barons you see before you, clad in mail, are bent on destroying me and obliterating my kingdom, nay our whole nation. They do not believe that we can survive. They glory in their war-horses and equipment. For us, the name of the Lord must be our hope of victory in battle. This day is a day of rejoicing: the birthday of John the Baptist. With our Lord Jesus as commander, Saint Andrew and the martyr Saint Thomas shall fight today with the saints of Scotland for the honour of their country and their nation. If you heartily repent for your sins you will be victorious, under God's command.'

With these words ringing in their ears Bruce's men prepared for the coming fight.

Thus were they ready on either side,
And Englishmen with great pride
That were in the vanguard . . .
Their horse with spurs hardened they
And galloped at them sturdily,
And they [the Scots] met them right hardily.

As Edward's army progressed slowly across the carse, all became conscious of movement up on the tree-lined ridge to their left, in the direction of the New Park. Then out from the forest canopy emerged the Scottish host, Carrick's brigade leading, Moray's and Douglas's on either flank. Bruce for the moment kept his own brigade in reserve and out of sight.

No sooner had they emerged than each man knelt down and prayed. 'What!', exclaimed the excitable Edward, 'Those men kneel to ask for mercy.' 'You are right', ventured one of his lieutenants, Sir Ingram de Umfraville, adding 'they ask for mercy, but not from you. They ask it from God.' The Scots, arising as one from their orisons, advanced slowly down the hill and onto the carse. And there they halted and formed their schiltrons. Once the great circles of spears were in place, the sergeants ceased barking out

The Scottish schiltrons engage with the English cavalry on Day Two. The triangular shield (left) bears the arms of Sir Marmaduke Tweng, a veteran of Stirling Bridge, who at Bannockburn surrendered to Bruce personally and was subsequently freed without ransom.

The two armies engage on Day Two. The English vanguard, led by the Earl of Gloucester (arms: three red chevrons), crashes into Carrick's brigade. Gloucester's hasty charge hindered the English archers from firing their deadly arrows into the vulnerable schiltron.

their orders. An eerie silence descended, broken only by the snorting of a horse here, a clank of armour there.

The sight was too tempting for Gloucester, despite the events of the previous day. He turned the vanguard through 90 degrees, snapped his visor shut, couched his lance close to his ribs, pricked his spurs into his horse's side and galloped full-tilt up the slope towards Carrick's schiltron. The vanguard followed in hot pursuit. Within moments they were upon the forest of spears. Gloucester was among the first to be unhorsed and killed, whether pierced by a Scottish spear or crushed beneath the great hooves of the heavy destriers will never be known. The carnage wrought by that murderous first

impact also ended Clifford's earthly existence, and Tiptoft's and Mauley's and Sir John Comyn's, son of the guardian killed by Bruce in 1306. They were first among the many casualties the English army would suffer that day.

Gloucester's hot-headed action was the catalyst for all-out battle. Edward's main force likewise wheeled to the left, gathered itself and charged at Moray and Douglas's flanking schiltrons – to similar effect. The dreadful sounds of clashing metal and neighing horses, shouting men and anguished cries filled the warm June air. Somehow the English archers, dispersed by Gloucester's foolhardy charge, regrouped and began firing their deadly armament into the schiltrons,

though as their arrows rained down from the skies, as many shot into the backs of their own knights as into the enemy. Bruce, acutely aware of the threat they posed, ordered Keith and his cavalry to run them down. They did their job perfectly, scattering them to the four winds.

It was now that Bruce showed his general's worth. Scenting victory, he seized the moment and slipped the leash off his own brigade. Angus Óg MacDonald of the Isles and his men rampaged screaming down the slope, presaging the famous Highland Charge that would one day be feared across the world. Crashing into the mêlée, they helped force the English ever nearer the boggy ground below the carse.

In their excitement, even the peasants guarding the Scottish supplies joined in, armed with anything that came to hand. Thinking them to be yet more reinforcements, the English finally turned tail and fled, as best they could, across the intractable ground between the Bannock Burn and the Forth's muddy tidal flats. Many were drowned. Others were cut down by their pursuers or by their own comrades desperate to get away. So full of dead and dying bodies was the Bannock Burn that it was said a man could cross without getting his feet wet. By the end of the day, one English earl, over 40 English knights and countless more unnamed Englishmen lay dead on the field of battle.

Thus ended the great Battle of Bannockburn.

The Earl of Gloucester was among the first English knights to die that day. The Earl of Pembroke (blue & white hoops) managed to return to King Edward and lead him from the battlefield when it was obvious all was lost.

EPILOGUE

King Robert now was right at his height
For each day then grew his might,
His men waxed rich and his country
Abounded well with corn and fee [land].

Edward II was murdered at Berkeley Castle, Gloucestershire, in 1327, and laid to rest in Gloucester Cathedral. Right up to his death, he refused to acknowledge Bruce as king, or Scotland as independent. Nothing – not even the humiliation of losing Berwick (1318) or his near-capture by Bruce in Yorkshire (1322) – could dissuade him of his folly.

Somehow, amid all the chaos of battle, King Edward contrived to escape, escorted from the field by the Earl of Pembroke and Sir Giles d'Argentan. Leaving his sovereign in Pembroke's safekeeping, Sir Giles returned to the fray, and there he too lay down his life.

In the fading light, Bruce walked amongst the debris of battle. And there he found his nephew, Gilbert de Clare, Earl of Gloucester, the young man's yellow and red surcoat stained with blood. Bruce had his corpse carried from the field and taken to the kirk of St. Ninian, north of the New Park beside the road leading to Stirling Castle. And there he remained all night in vigil, lamenting the loss of his beloved kinsman.

Meanwhile, Edward and his escort rode furiously back along the road to Edinburgh, stopping only briefly at Winchburgh to feed and water their horses. Despite being hotly pursued by Douglas and around 60 horse, they managed to make it to Dunbar, where Edward took ship for the comparative safety of Berwick Castle, which he reached on 27 June. A fortnight later he crept back into England.

Others fleeing the battlefield weren't so fortunate. The Earl of Hereford with a considerable cavalry force sped towards Lanark, reaching Bothwell Castle on the Clyde, then in English hands, late that same night. By morning they found themselves trapped, for Carrick and his men had tracked them across country and laid siege to the stronghold. Its keeper, Walter Fitzgilbert, realising all was lost, surrendered his charge. Bruce rejoiced at the news and made full use of the handsome ransoms available, for sheltering therein, along with Hereford, were Robert de Umfraville, Earl of Angus, Maurice lord of Berkeley, John lord of Segrave, Anthony de Lucy and others. Hereford alone was exchanged for Bruce's queen Elizabeth, his sister Mary, his daughter the lady Marjorie, and old Robert Wishart, Bishop of Glasgow, who had supported Bruce from the outset in 1306. Fitzgilbert, a Scot, entered Bruce's peace, as did his counterpart at Stirling Castle, Sir Philip Mowbray. Bruce had both fortresses 'razed to the ground', thus sharing the same fate that befell Roxburgh and Edinburgh in the build-up to the great battle.

Until his dying day, Edward stubbornly refused to recognise his adversary as rightful king of Scotland. He even had the audacity to in

invade again, in the summer of 1322. In the end it was not the Scots who finally 'did' for Edward; he was undone by his own nobles, murdered when a red-hot spit was thrust into his bowels. His bones had lain in the ground barely six months when his son and successor, Edward III, concluded the business left unfinished at Bannockburn.

On 17 March 1328, in a chamber within the precincts of the monastery of St. Mary the Virgin at Holyrood, downhill from his great castle of Edinburgh, Bruce affixed his seal to the Treaty of Edinburgh. Among all the many clauses and legal jargon, one phrase would have shone bright into the aging king's eyes:

' . . . We [the English Crown] will and concede . . . that the kingdom of Scotland shall remain for ever separate in all respects from the kingdom of England, free and in peace, without any subjection, servitude, claim or demand, with its rightful boundaries as they were held and reserved in the times of Alexander of good memory king of Scotland last deceased, to the magnificent prince, the lord Robert, by God's grace illustrious king of Scots.'

As he read those words, Bruce would have reflected on all the years of hardship and sacrifice that had gone before. But most of all he would have relived those two days in June 1314 – the vigil and feast day of the Nativity of St. John the Baptist – when he led his people to their greatest victory over the 'auld enemy'. The battle of Bannockburn may not have formally secured Bruce's place on the throne of Scotland, or brought an end to the bloody Wars of Independence, but what it did achieve was the

unqualified support by the Scots for Bruce as their sovereign king, after years of bitter internecine rivalry with the Balliols. For Bruce, the great battle of Bannockburn had been the defining moment of his illustrious reign.

A! Freedom is a noble thing
Freedom lets man have liking [pleasure].
Freedom to man all solace gives,
He lives at ease who freely lives.

King Robert Bruce celebrates victory at Bannockburn; William Findlay's Liberation of Scotland, *depicts Bruce in his finest hour, above a female figure representing Scotia, being defended by noble warriors.*

FURTHER READING

All the quotations in this book are taken from John Barbour's epic poem *The Bruce*. Composed in the 1370s, it is the earliest account of King Robert Bruce's life and reign, and includes a blow-by-blow account of the battle of Bannockburn. The original text, together with a modern translation, is available in A. A. M. Duncan (ed.) *John Barbour, The Bruce* (Canongate 1997).

The most definitive modern biography of King Robert Bruce is Geoffrey Barrow's masterly *Robert Bruce & The Community of the Realm of Scotland* (Edinburgh University Press 1988). This includes the most insightful, up-to-date, account of the battle of Bannockburn available.

The following books focus more specifically on the armies and personalities involved, including their tactics, armour and weapons: Armstrong, P. & Turner, G. *Bannockburn 1314: Robert Bruce's great victory* (Oxford, 2002); Nusbacher, A. S. *The Battle of Bannockburn 1314* (Tempus, 2002); Rothero, C. *The Scottish and Welsh Wars 1250-1400* (Osprey Men-at-Arms Series 151, 1989)

Finally, there are Nigel Tranter's three historical novels on the life of King Robert Bruce - *The Steps to the Empty Throne* (1969), *The Path of the Hero King* (1970), and *The Price of the King's Peace* (1971), republished in omnibus edition as *The Bruce Trilogy* (Coronet, 1985).

Author: **CHRIS TABRAHAM** is Principal Historian for Historic Scotland, the government agency charged with the care of hundreds of historic sites across Scotland. He holds a degree in Ancient and Medieval History and Archaeology, has excavated widely across Scotland, and is the author of numerous books, including *The Illustrated History of Scotland*, also published by Lomond Books, and most recently *Clan and Castle: The Lives and Lands of Scotland's Great Families*, published by Historic Scotland. He lives in East Lothian.

ACKNOWLEDGEMENTS

I am grateful to my colleague at Historic Scotland, Peter Yeoman, for his helpful comments on the text.

First published in Great Britain in 2009 by
Lomond Books Ltd., 14 Freskyn Place,
East Mains Industrial Estate, Broxburn EH52 5NF
www.lomondbooks.com

Produced by Colin Baxter Photography Ltd
Copyright © Colin Baxter Photography Ltd 2009

Text © Chris Tabraham 2009

ISBN 978-1-84204-183-3

Printed in China

Pictures © 2009 All Rights Reserved by:

akg-images / British Library: page 1

Iain Masterson / Alamy: page 2

Angelo Hornak Photo Library: page 30
    (Courtesy of the Dean and Chapter, Gloucester Cathedral)

British Library Board. Licence No. COLBAX01: pages 7, 10, 12

Barryob from Wikimedia Commons: page 14 left

Colin Baxter: pages 8, 11

Colin Baxter Photography: pages 23, 25

David Robertson / Alamy: page 4

Glasgow Museums and Art Galleries / Licensor
    www.scran.ac.uk: page 26, 31

Hunterian Museum and Art Gallery, University of Glasgow /
    Licensor www.scran.ac.uk: page 13 bottom

Ipankonin from Wikimedia Commons: page 14 right

The London Art Archive / Alamy: page 6;

The Master and Fellows of Corpus Christi College, Cambridge: page 21

Mark Churms: Front cover, pages 15, 28-29, BATTLE OF BANNOCKBURN – Scotland 1314 © MarkChurms.com 1994 (revised 2004); page 16 IN SINGLE COMBAT – Bannockburn 1314 © MarkChurms.com 1992; page 24, 1314 – Robert The Bruce, Scotland 1314A.D. © MarkChurms.com 2006

National Museums of Scotland / Licensor
    www.scran.ac.uk: pages 13 top, 22

National Trust for Scotland / Licensor www.scran.ac.uk: pages 18, 19

Private Collection / Licensor www.scran.ac.uk: back cover

Scottish National Portrait Gallery: page 20

Stirling Smith Art Gallery & Museum / Licensor
    www.scran.ac.uk: page 27

Front Cover: Battle of Bannockburn (detail), by Mark Churms   *Back Cover:* Bruce slays Sir Henry de Bohun, stained glass design
Page 1: Battle of Bannockburn, from the Holkham Bible c. 1325-1350